CW00722207

JUST TO SAY

HOW MUCH

I LOVE YOU

X X y

X Y

X

To:

Carolann

From:

MUM xxxxx

ISBN: 0-88396-943-2

Certain trademarks are used under license.

Manufactured in China.
First Printing: 2005

✺ This book is printed on recycled paper.

Blue Mountain Arts, Inc.
P.O. Box 4549, Boulder, Colorado 80306

A Little Bit of...

Love for You,

Daughter

Blue Mountain Arts®
Boulder, Colorado

Daughter,
You Are
Life's Greatest
Gift to Me

Memories come flooding
over me as I look
back on the years.
I want to hold on to you
and at the same time
watch you fly high
and free...

It's so easy to remember
your very first steps
and how I held out
my hand for you
to hold.
As each year passes,
you take more steps,
and some of these will
eventually lead you
away from me.

But always remember that
my hand and my heart
are here for you.
You will always be
my daughter.
You have been life's
greatest gift to me,
and I love you so much.

— Vickie M. Worsham

A Few Words from My Heart to Yours, Daughter…

In your happiest and
most exciting moments,
my heart will celebrate
and smile beside you.
In your lowest lows, my
love will be there to keep
you warm, to give you
strength, and to remind
you that your sunshine
is sure to come again…

In your moments of accomplishment, I will be filled so full of pride that I may have a hard time keeping the feeling inside of me.

In your moments of
disappointment, I will
be a shoulder to cry on,
a hand to hold, and a
love that will gently
enfold you until
everything's okay...

In your life, I wish I could give you a very special gift. It would be this: When you look in the mirror in the days ahead, may you find yourself smiling a hundred times more than frowning at what you see.

Smile because you know
that a loving, capable,
sensible, strong, precious
person is reflected there.
And when you look at me,
may you remember how
very much I love you...
and how much I'll
always care.

— Laurel Atherton

No one could have
   prepared me
For the depth of love
That sprang into my heart
The moment you were born.
You become dearer to me
With every year
   that passes.

— Cheryl Barker

Even if a day
should go by
when I don't say
"I love you…"
May never a moment
go by without your
knowing I do.

— Daniel Haughian

I'm So Proud
of You

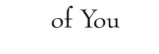

Daughter, you have
   always been
a wonderful source of
   joy to me.
You have touched my life
with a magic all
   your own...

You are more than a
dream come true
for me:
you are a part of my life
that will carry on.
And as I watch you
changing,
I see a special happiness
in all that you do.

With my heart full of
memories,
I want you to know that
the love we share
has made being a parent
the greatest feeling
I have ever known.

— Deanna Beisser

You are a shining
example of what a
daughter can be —
loving and compassionate
beautiful and good
honest and principled
determined and
    independent
sensitive and intelligent

You are a shining
example of what every
parent wishes their
daughter were
and I am so very
proud of
you

— Susan Polis Schutz

Daughter,
Your Happiness
Is What I
Wish for Most

I wish for you to always see the goodness in this world, to do your part in helping those less fortunate, to walk hand in hand with those of less talent, and to be an equal with those who are different…

I wish for you the
  self-confidence to say no
  when it is necessary and
  the strength to stand
  alone.
I wish for you the approval
  of yourself to love and
  respect everything that
  you are and will become.

I wish for you to reap the
fruits of your talents
and walk with pride
down the road of life.
Most of all, I wish for you
to be happy, for then
you'll have the key that
will open all the world's
doors to you.

— Jackie Olson

I Love
Having You
for My
Daughter

I looked at you today
and saw the same
beautiful eyes
that looked at me
with love
when you were a baby...

I looked at you today
and saw the same
   beautiful mouth
that made me cry when
   you first smiled
      at me
when you were a baby

I looked at you today
and saw my beautiful
   daughter
no longer a baby
but a beautiful person
with a full range of
   emotions and feelings
and ideas and goals...

Every day is exciting
as I continue to watch
    you grow
And I want you to always
    know that
in good and in bad times
I will love you
and that no matter what
    you do...

or how you think
or what you say
you can depend on
my support, guidance
friendship and love
every minute of every day
I love being your mother

— Susan Polis Schutz

There are gifts that are
far above priceless.
There are memories that
are made of pure love.
There are special miracles
that really do come true.

And all my life, you
will always be…
a wonderful gift,
a treasure of memories,
and an amazing
miracle… to me.

— Douglas Pagels

A Daughter
Is a Wonderful
Blessing

A daughter's smile is a
   sight that you treasure
   each time you see it
And the sound of her
   laughter always brings
   joy to your heart
Her successes mean more
   to you than your own
And her happiness is your
   happiness…

Daughters aren't perfect, but you, Daughter, come close
You have given me more happiness than you know
I am thankful for your kindness and thoughtfulness
And I am proud of who you are and how you live your life

Words can't express how
   much you mean to me
   or how much I love you
The love goes too deep,
   and the gratitude and
   pride I feel are boundless
Thank you for blessing my
   life in so many ways

— Barbara Cage

I Am Always
Here for You,
Daughter…

When you need someone
to talk to
I hope you will
talk to me
When you need someone
to laugh with
I hope you will
laugh with me...

When you need someone
to advise you
I hope you will
turn to me
When you need someone
to help you
I hope you will
let me help you

I cherish and love
everything about you —
my beautiful daughter
And I will always
   support you
as a mother, as a person
and as a friend

— Susan Polis Schutz

I Think of You
Every Day

You probably don't realize how important you are to me. There are times when the one thing that helps me get through the day... is thinking of you...

You are so important to me. You make me think, you make me laugh, you make me feel alive. You put things in perspective for me. You provide support and encouragement, you lessen my worries, and you increase my joys.

If my life were a puzzle,
you would be the one piece
that was a perfect fit.

Every day...
I think of you.
And I've got a million
smiles to prove it.

— Marin McKay

Thank You,
Daughter,
for Giving Me
Happiness
and Smiles

You are a blessing that I'm forever thankful for.
I love being with you,
and every time we're apart
there's a little part of me
that stays with you...

Your sense of humor
  delights me.
Your laughter is one of
  my favorite sounds,
and your smiles light up
  my heart.
I'm so proud of you
and the kind of person
  you are.

I love you,
and I want you to know
that being your parent
has been one of my
   greatest joys.

— Barbara Cage

Wherever
You Go in Life,
Daughter,
My Love Will
Be with You

I love you so much.
I want you to remember
that... every single day.
And I want you to know
that these are things I'll
always hope and pray...

I'll always hope and pray that the world will treat you fairly. That people will appreciate the one-in-a-million person you are. That you will be safe, smart, and sure to make good choices on your journey through life…

That a wealth of opportunities will come your way. That your blessings will be many, your troubles will be few, and that life will be very generous in giving you all the happiness and success you deserve...

You're not just a fantastic daughter. You're a rare and extraordinary person. All the different facets of your life — the ones you reveal to the rest of the world, and the ones known only to those you're close to — are so impressive.

And as people look even deeper, I know they can't help but see how wonderful you are inside.

I'll always love you with all my heart. And I couldn't be more proud of you... if I tried.

— Douglas Pagels

We wish to thank Susan Polis Schutz for
permission to reprint the following poems
that appear in this publication: "I looked at
you today," "You are a shining example," and
"When you need someone…." Copyright ©
1986, 1994, 1996 by Stephen Schutz and
Susan Polis Schutz. All rights reserved.